What Was the Age of the Dinosaurs?

by Megan Stine

illustrated by Gregory Copeland

SCHOLASTIC INC.

For Travis—MS

To Father Paul, with apologies—GC

ISBN 978-1-338-28311-2

12 11 10 9 8 7 6 5   18 19 20 21 22 23

Printed in the U.S.A.   40

First Scholastic printing, January 2018

Contents

What Was the Age of the Dinosaurs?

In 1822, a young country doctor named Gideon Mantell was living in Sussex, England. He delivered babies and treated people with serious diseases.

Gideon Mantell

But Mantell had another passion as well. Ever since childhood, he had loved to collect fossils—the ancient remains of dead plants and animals. Whenever he could, the busy doctor spent time digging near the chalky cliffs of England's coastline. At first what he dug up were small pieces of fossil bones. But as time went on, he began to find some big bones—really big ones. The bones were too big to belong to any known animal. Even elephant bones would have been smaller.

Then one day, Mantell's wife, Mary, found a few enormous fossil teeth. She brought them to her husband.

What were they? What kind of animal could possibly have teeth as big as this?

Mantell wasn't sure what to think. He talked to other scientists. No one could agree about what they were. A man named William Buckland had once been given some huge bones. He studied them for six years and finally decided they belonged to a giant lizard no one had ever seen before. Buckland called it *Megalosaurus* (say: MEG-uh-lo-SORE-us), which means "big lizard."

Megalosaurus

Mantell asked Buckland about the huge teeth he had found. But Buckland didn't think they had come from a creature similar to his *Megalosaurus*. He said they came from a fish!

After that, Mantell went to a museum and looked at other fossils and animal skeletons on display. The teeth he had found looked exactly like iguana teeth—only many times larger. If they came from an iguana, it would have to have been at least sixty feet long! That's as long as a house!

Suddenly Mantell realized something exciting. Like Buckland, he had discovered a new kind of animal no one knew about. He decided to call it *Iguanodon* (ig-WAN-uh-don).

Iguanodon

Neither Mantell nor Buckland understood that they had stumbled onto a completely unknown group of animals. The word *dinosaur* hadn't been invented yet—and wouldn't be for another twenty years. But that's what *Megalosaurus* and *Iguanodon* were. In the early nineteenth century, no one yet realized that in prehistoric times, gigantic animals had roamed the earth. But soon, more fossils were found, and slowly scientists began to put together the pieces of a long-lost world—the Age of the Dinosaurs.

How Fossils Form

When a plant or animal dies in a watery environment, it quickly becomes buried in mud and silt. Soon the soft tissue rots away, leaving just the hard bones or shells behind. Over time these are covered by more layers of earth, which harden into rock and encase the remains—the fossil.

Scientists who study fossils are called paleontologists (PAY-lee-on-TAH-lo-jists). (The name comes from the word *paleo*, which means ancient or from earth's long-ago past.)

CHAPTER 1
The Prehistoric World

Two hundred thirty million years ago, the Age of the Dinosaurs began. The first baby dinosaurs poked their heads out of their eggshells and looked around for something to eat.

The earth was a very different place then. North America didn't exist. Neither did Africa or Europe. All seven continents we know today were clumped together into one huge landmass that we call Pangaea (pan-JEE-uh).

Pangaea was surrounded on all sides by water. The center of the huge continent was a hot desert, where not much could survive. A giant ocean covered the rest of the earth. Near the coastlines, the ocean cooled the air. Cool air and water made it possible for fabulous life-forms to develop.

Pangaea

Ferns grew along the coast. Moss covered the rocks. There were forests of pine trees and palm trees. Spiders and beetles crawled about.

The ocean was full of life. There were huge swimming reptiles—animals like lizards and turtles, only bigger. Some, called ichthyosaurs (ICK-thee-oh-sores), looked much more like dolphins or fish. They were predators that hunted fish. Others, called plesiosaurs (PLEE-see-oh-sores), were more like gigantic shell-less turtles with incredibly long necks. They may have eaten baby ichthyosaurs for lunch.

Ichthyosaurs

Plesiosaur

Reptiles also dominated the land at that time. There were none of the animals we know today—no dogs, cats, giraffes, monkeys, or apes. There weren't even any birds—and definitely no people! It was mostly a reptile's world, although the ancient reptiles were not the same reptiles we know today.

This was the beginning of a time period called the Mesozoic era. It began 250 million years ago—or 250 "mya," as scientists say. It lasted until the dinosaurs died out, around 65 mya.

The Mesozoic era is divided up into three parts—Triassic, Jurassic, and Cretaceous. The very first dinosaurs appeared on earth during the last part of the Triassic, about 230 mya. Dinosaurs existed on earth for about 165 million years.

When exactly did the first dinosaur appear? It's hard to say for sure, because dinosaurs evolved from other reptiles over millions of years. But the earliest dinosaur was probably *Eoraptor* (EE-oh-RAP-tor)—a small animal weighing between eight and twenty-two pounds. With jagged teeth, long legs, and long claws, it was a small, quick, deadly predator. It lived in the forest, where it chased and captured smaller creatures. It probably ate plants, too.

Eoraptor

As millions of years went by, different kinds of dinosaurs came into being. How did that happen? The answer lies in evolution.

Evolution is the name for changes that occur in living things over time. Charles Darwin was a scientist in the nineteenth century who studied nature. He wrote a famous book about the idea of evolution. Darwin said that, in each species, some would survive longer than others. It was not just

Charles Darwin

a matter of luck. Those that survived were the best suited to thrive in the world. They lived long enough to have babies that would be born with the same strong traits. Animals of the same species without those traits didn't live as long. In time, they died out.

Darwin explained that over thousands and millions of years, all kinds of species developed—including human beings, who evolved from ape-like creatures.

Species

What is a species? It is a group of animals that have many common characteristics. To be within the same species, the animals in the group must also be able to mate with each other and have babies who can later have more babies. A poodle and a Labrador retriever are both dogs. They may not look much alike, but they do belong to the same species, *Canis lupus familiaris*. That's because both of these kinds of dogs can have puppies together, which in turn can have puppies of their own.

A poodle, a Labrador retriever, and a labradoodle

CHAPTER 2
The First Dinosaurs

Most of the first dinosaurs were small pet-size creatures. But over millions of years, bigger dinosaurs began to appear on earth. One Triassic dinosaur—

Herrerasaurus (huh-RARE-uh-SORE-us)—was fifteen feet long and weighed 450 pounds. That's not very big, compared to dinosaurs that came later. But it was a lot bigger than *Eoraptor.* When *Herrerasaurus* wondered what was for dinner, *Eoraptor* may have been the answer!

Herrerasaurus

In the Triassic period, many of the dinosaurs were predators—they chased and killed other creatures for food. Some of them had snaggly hooked teeth. They might have used their teeth like fishhooks, to catch fish. Some Triassic dinosaurs ate both animals and plants.

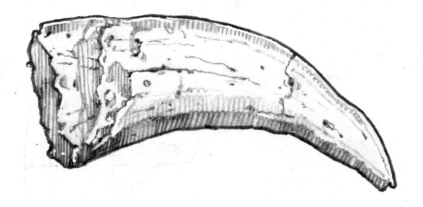

As millions of years went by, the huge continent called Pangaea slowly broke apart. By the end of the Triassic, it was splitting into two separate continents—one in the north and one in the south. Dinosaurs lived in both areas.

Now that there were two continents, there were more coastlines. The weather changed. There was more rain, so plants could grow bigger. The animals had more food.

Everything, in fact, was about to change.

The Jurassic world was about to begin.

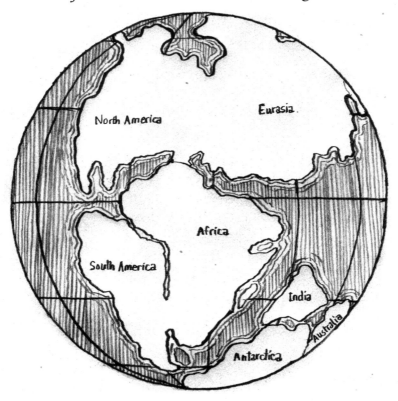

Pangaea splitting into separate continents

CHAPTER 3
The Jurassic World

The Jurassic period began 200 mya and lasted about 55 million years. The world didn't look the same that whole time. During the Jurassic, the continents continued to break apart. Plants and animals continued to evolve. Ferns and trees grew taller. Now there were lush rain forests with lots of food for bigger animals to eat. But the food was up high—the leaves were at the tops of tall trees. So dinosaurs with long necks probably had a better chance to survive. Over time, some of the biggest dinosaurs with the longest necks evolved during the Jurassic period.

Brachiosaurus (BRAK-ee-oh-SORE-us) was one of them. It lived in what is now North America during the last part of the Jurassic. At eighty or more feet long, the dinosaur was about the length of two school buses! It had spoon-shaped teeth that were good for scraping leaves from branches. *Brachiosaurus* needed to eat about 260 pounds of leaves every day! Can you imagine how much poop it made?

It's amazing to think that vegetarian dinosaurs grew bigger than the vicious meat-eaters—but it's true!

How Dinosaurs Are Named

Dinosaurs usually have two names, like *Tyrannosaurus rex*. The first name is called the genus name. It tells you what kind of dinosaur it is. The second name is the species name.

In the past, scientists tried to name dinosaurs based on their appearance. *Brachiosaurus* means "arm lizard." It got this name because of its long forelegs. But often in the past, the names given turned out to be wrong. *Oviraptor* (OH-vuh-RAP-tor) means "egg thief." It got this name because an oviraptor was found near a nest. But oviraptors don't steal eggs—they sit on them. Still, the name stuck!

Today, a new species is often named for the place where its fossils were found or for the person who found them. It's the custom to make the names sound like Greek or Latin. That's why they're so hard to pronounce.

Oviraptor

The Jurassic world was home to many different kinds of dinosaurs. One of the most famous North American dinosaurs was the brontosaurus (BRON-tuh-SORE-us). It lived in the area that became Wyoming, Utah, and Colorado, and roamed around eating every plant in sight. With huge, thick legs, it may have been able to knock down the trees it wanted to eat!

Diplodocus (di-PLOH-dock-us) was a huge plant-eater with a row of spines on its tail. If a larger meat-eating dinosaur came near, diplodocus could swing its tail around like a bullwhip!

Were there any meat-eaters in North America that could threaten a diplodocus or brontosaurus? Yes. The fiercest predator during the Jurassic was the allosaurus (AL-oh-SORE-us). It only weighed about one and a half tons and was twenty-eight feet long—nowhere near as big as a diplodocus.

But it had jagged teeth and sharp claws that could rip another dinosaur's throat out. Many bones of plant-eaters have been found with bite marks in them from allosaurus teeth.

There were small meat-eaters during the Jurassic, too. *Compsognathus* (comp-SOG-nah-thus) was one. It lived in the area of what is now Germany and France, and was one of the smallest dinosaurs ever. Compsognathus was about four feet long—but most of its length was in the tail. The body, neck, and head were only about two feet long. At around five pounds, it weighed only slightly more than a roasted chicken. What did it eat? Likely lizards and other small animals. It also may have eaten a creature called *Archaeopteryx* (ar-kee-OP-tur-ix)—which might have been the first bird.

During the Jurassic, the seas were still full of long-necked plesiosaurs. They had been around since the Triassic period, and they would last through the entire Age of the Dinosaurs.

Dinosaurs with spikes, plates, and feathers first showed up during the Jurassic, too. Stegosaurus (STEG-oh-SORE-us) was a plant-eater that lived

in the area that became Colorado, Utah, and Wyoming. It had pointy, fan-shaped plates along its back. The plates looked like armor, but they were actually too soft to do any damage to other dinosaurs. The plates might have changed colors. Maybe that helped stegosaurs find each other when they were ready to mate. Stegosaurus had a tiny head and very small brain. As a species, they didn't last very long. Stegosaurs were "only" around for 30 million years or so. They became extinct long before the rest of the dinosaurs did.

As time went on, there would be hundreds of different kinds of dinosaurs—small scampering animals and huge killing machines. But the most famous—and most brutal—dinosaur of all time didn't appear in the Jurassic period.

No, the world had to change some more before *T. rex* would appear.

CHAPTER 4
Rulers of the World

In movies it seems like all the most interesting dinosaurs lived in the Jurassic period. But the Jurassic wasn't the high point in the Age of the Dinosaurs. The most ferocious and most famous dinosaur of all time—*Tyrannosaurus rex* (tu-RAN-uh-SORE-us rex)—didn't show up until the Cretaceous (cree-TAY-shus) period. *Cretaceous* is not an easy word to read, spell, or say. No wonder Hollywood didn't use it!

The Cretaceous was the time when dinosaurs truly ruled the world.

Why?

Everything about life in the Cretaceous suited dinosaurs. The continents had broken apart more. By the end of the Cretaceous, the globe looked almost like it does today. North America, South America, Africa, and Eurasia were all separate continents.

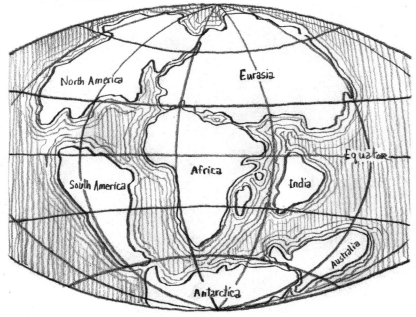

The continents at the end of the Cretaceous

How Can Continents Move?

Over time—millions of years—the earth is always changing. Volcanoes erupt. Earthquakes split sections of the land apart. Mountains are formed. All of these things happen because the earth's shell isn't solid. It's made up of movable platforms, called tectonic plates. Little by little, as the plates move, the land changes shape. The earth continues to change, and the continents keep drifting apart, even today.

Rift from an earthquake

As the earth changed shape, the weather continued to change—and it was different in the northern and southern parts of the world. New kinds of plants began to grow. It's believed that for the first time ever, there were flowers.

Still, the Cretaceous landscape didn't look like the world does today. There were more ferns and pine forests than we have now. It was hotter than it is now. The air was moist in many places. Dinosaurs thrived in the hot, wet environment.

With more plants to eat, the biggest plant-eating dinosaurs evolved. Titanosaurs first appeared in the Jurassic period and existed all through the Cretaceous period. They were similar to brachiosaurs, only bigger.

Titanosaur

The bones of a new species of titanosaur were found in 2011. They were found by a farm worker in Patagonia at the southern tip of South America. Just the thigh bone alone was taller than a man! The newly discovered dinosaur was 122 feet long and 65 feet tall. That's longer than a professional basketball court. It probably weighed about eighty-five tons. Scientists haven't named this new species of titanosaur yet. When they do, they'll likely choose a name that honors the region and the farm owners who discovered it.

During the Cretaceous period, dinosaurs evolved into many different forms. Some had spikes on their heads, or crowns of frilly feathers. Some had wings. Many dinosaurs were covered in feathers.

With more plant-eaters roaming the earth, there were more animals for the meat-eaters to prey on, so all the dinosaurs ate very well.

The Cretaceous lasted almost 80 million years. During that time, a number of different small mammals appeared. Mammals are a group of animals (including dogs, cats, elephants, mice, and human beings) whose babies are born alive—mammals don't lay eggs. There were still no large mammals, but tiny creatures like mice appeared, eating bugs and living in the trees.

Maotherium, a Cretaceous mammal

Birds took to the skies during this time period, too. There were also giant flying reptiles, called pterosaurs (TARE-oh-sores). The biggest one known was a predator called *Quetzalcoatlus* (KET-zel-ko-WAT-lus). It had a wingspan of almost forty feet! Imagine a huge, hungry animal with a long pointy beak. It soars over your head, then swoops down for the kill. *Quetzalcoatlus* was bigger than a small airplane—and it would have wanted to eat you!

Dragons in the Sky, Monsters in the Seas

In China, people have told stories about dragons for thousands of years. For many centuries, dragons have appeared in Chinese artwork as a symbol of strength. Why? Early Chinese people may have found pterosaur skeletons. Or they may have found remains of velociraptors (veh-LA-suh-RAP-tors), which look a lot like dragons. Since they didn't know about dinosaurs and pterosaurs,

Velociraptor

people might have made up stories about these fantastic beasts.

In Scotland, there have long been stories about a creature called the Loch Ness monster, which supposedly lives in a lake. The monster is said to be a huge serpent—like a long-necked plesiosaur.

Scientists don't believe the Loch Ness monster ever existed. But it's easy to see where the myth might have come from. At one time, giant long-necked sea creatures did exist. The bones from an ancient plesiosaur may have sparked someone's fears—or imagination.

Another fearsome dinosaur from the Cretaceous period was the *Utahraptor* (YU-tah-RAP-tor). It lived in the American West. It was twenty-three feet long and eight feet tall. That's so big, it would barely fit in most people's living

rooms. *Utahraptor* had huge claws on its toes. It would chase down its prey, then use its claws to rip its victim to shreds. Or it may have pinned the other animal down while it tore off hunks of flesh.

Utahraptors were more than twice as big as velociraptors, which lived in what is now Mongolia. But velociraptors were plenty fierce. One set of dinosaur bones has been found that shows a battle to the death between a velociraptor and another dinosaur called protoceratops (pro-toh-SER-a-tops). The protoceratops was an eight-foot-long creature with a huge head, a frilled collar, strong

rear legs, and a parrotlike beak. Both skeletons were preserved at the moment they died—in killing positions. The velociraptor's clawed foot is jammed right into the protoceratops's neck!

But the fiercest dinosaur of all time evolved toward the end of the Cretaceous—the end of the Age of the Dinosaurs.

It was *Tyrannosaurus rex.*

CHAPTER 5
Here Comes *T. rex*!

Tyrannosaurus rex was the king of the Cretaceous period. It was an incredible killing machine that lived in what we know as the North American West. In terms of brute strength, *T. rex* was the strongest killer ever. It had an enormous and powerful jaw and the biggest teeth of any carnivorous dinosaur. A young *T. rex*'s teeth were shaped like knife blades. When *T. rex* grew up, its teeth became cone-shaped. Some were as big as bananas!

The real power behind the *T. rex* was the force of its bite—more than three times stronger than that of a great white shark! What made it so strong? Not just its big jaw. *T. rex* had a huge neck bone that gave it the strength to bite very deeply into its prey.

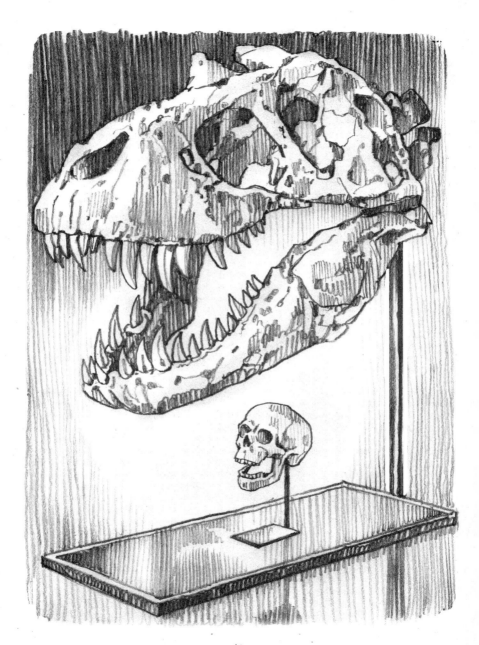

The muscle power in *T. rex*'s jaw and the size of its huge head earned it the title of "king." (*Rex* means "king" in Latin.) It was also the king of dinosaurs because it was the largest predator in North America at that time. It could kill dinosaurs that weighed two or three times as much as it did. Triceratops (try-SAIR-uh-tops), the three-horned dinosaur, was one of its victims. Triceratops was a plant-eater that was

about thirty feet long and weighed ten tons. Some triceratops bones have been found with *T. rex* bite marks in them.

T. rexes and other meat-eaters may have hunted together in packs, like wolves. The smaller *T. rexes* were probably faster than their parents. Although the parents had more powerful jaws for killing, the younger dinosaurs may have been better at chasing down prey. Teamwork!

Giganotosaurus (ji-GAN-oh-toe-SORE-us), whose remains are found in present-day South America, was an even bigger predator than *T. rex.*

Giganotosaurus

It weighed almost eight tons and stood forty-three feet long. It had a bigger jaw than a *T. rex*, too—big enough to eat a man in a single bite!

Did *T. rex* and *Giganotosaurus* ever fight each other? No. Besides coming from different continents, they lived during different times in the Cretaceous period. Remember, the period was almost 80 million years long.

The Cretaceous was

T. rex

an amazing time—it spanned millions of years of dinosaur evolution. Over that time, duck-billed dinosaurs came into being. They were plant-eaters with hundreds of teeth in their mouths, all lined up in rows. These dinosaurs could replace their teeth anytime they fell out!

One of the fastest dinosaurs also appeared during the Cretaceous. Called *Dromiceiomimus* (dro-MEE-see-o-MYE-mus), it looked something like a huge ostrich with a long tail and arms.

Dromiceiomimus

Microraptor

And the smallest dinosaur appeared in this time period, too. *Microraptor* (MY-cro-RAP-tor) weighed only two pounds—about the size of a three-month-old kitten! *Microraptor* lived in what is now the country of China. It had feathers and four wings. It could probably fly or glide.

Some species of dinosaurs from earlier periods hung around for the entire Cretaceous. A group of meat-eating dinosaurs called abelisaurs (a-BEL-ah-SORES) lived throughout the period. Abelisaurs were fast on their feet—and vicious. They could chase down baby dinosaurs at high speeds—even baby titanosaurs—and eat them. Abelisaurs came in all sizes, from seventy pounds to several tons. With slender legs and long tails, they were more like giant alligators with ballerina legs!

Abelisaurs had the longest reign on earth of all the dinosaurs. As a group, they lasted from the early Jurassic to the end of the Cretaceous. That's about 118 million years.

Abelisaur

Of course no single dinosaur lived for millions of years. From birth to death, the smallest dinosaurs may have only lived a few years, while larger dinosaurs may have lived twenty or thirty years. The bigger, slow-moving ones could have lived for up to fifty years or more. But scientists don't know for sure, and some argue that the largest herbivores could have lived a century.

What did dinosaurs do all day? The big plant-eaters had to spend most of their time eating plants and trees. The meat-eaters spent most of their time hunting other creatures.

From the small size of their brains, we know that dinosaurs didn't think much. They didn't make decisions. They acted on instinct. (Instincts are ways of behaving that are inborn, not learned.) Dinosaurs' instincts told them to eat to stay alive.

Hunting, eating, sleeping. That was about it for the life of a dinosaur—except for one important thing. Dinosaurs had babies.

How Did Dinosaurs Sleep?

They must have rested or slept, but we don't know much about how most dinosaurs did it. It seems to have been impossible for a gigantic animal like *Titanosaurus* to lie down. In fact, if an animal that big ever fell over, the fall would kill it! It would crush itself with its own weight. But at least one dinosaur skeleton has been found in a sleeping position. *Mei long* was a small birdlike dinosaur found in China. It weighed about one pound, and stood about a foot tall. When the skeleton was discovered, the dinosaur had its snout tucked under one of its arms. Its legs were folded neatly under the body, just the way birds roost today. Chinese scientists found a second skeleton in the exact same position, more proof that it was a sleeping position. The dinosaurs were roosting when they died.

Skeleton of *Mei long* found in sleeping position

CHAPTER 6
Dinosaur Babies

Like reptiles and birds today, all dinosaurs laid eggs. Their eggs ranged from small to huge and came in various shapes. Some were ball shaped, like a grapefruit. Others were long narrow ovals, or shaped like footballs. Some eggs had ridges or bumps on the surface.

All dinosaur eggs were laid on the ground. Some were buried in mud. Others were placed in a bowl-shaped mud nest. Some dinosaurs laid their eggs in a circle, like the petals on a flower. Others may have buried their long eggs vertically in the ground.

The biggest dinosaur eggs ever found were twenty-one inches long. Those eggs didn't come from the biggest dinosaurs, though. They came from *Gigantoraptor* (ji-GAN-toe-RAP-tor). At more than a ton, *Gigantoraptor* was not small. But it was nowhere near as big as the very biggest plant-eaters—and their eggs weighed only two pounds each. A nest with *Gigantoraptor* eggs was found in the Gobi Desert. The nest was ten feet wide!

The smallest dinosaur eggs found so far are less than an inch in size. They were discovered in China. Scientists aren't sure, but they think the tiny eggs might have come from a *Microraptor*.

Did dinosaurs sit on their nests, the way birds do? Some did. Scientists know this because they have found fossilized nests with skeletons of adult dinosaurs sitting on top or nearby. One skeleton showed the dinosaur's feathered arms folded over the nest. It was an oviraptor. It may have

taken care of the babies after they hatched, too. Duck-billed dinosaurs probably tended their nests and fed the babies when they hatched. A duck-billed dinosaur found in Montana was named *Maiasaura* (MY-uh-SORE-uh), which means "good mother lizard." Why? This species appears to have stayed with the babies for a long time after they were born.

But the really big dinosaurs, like brontosaurus or diplodocus, are more likely to have laid their eggs and then walked away. Why? These dinosaurs were so big, they would have accidentally trampled on their own eggs or babies if they stuck around. It was better for the mother to get out of the way.

How big were the babies? *Argentinosaurus* (ar-jen-TEEN-uh-SORE-us) was one of the all-time biggest dinosaurs—as tall as a six-story building.

Its babies weighed about eleven pounds when they hatched—a lot more than most human children at birth. And they already had teeth.

A huge nest site was found in Patagonia in South America. The ground was covered with tens of thousands of eggs, over an area one square mile wide! Of course all those eggs didn't come from one dinosaur. Each dinosaur laid dozens of eggs. Scientists think that many dinosaurs used that same spot in Patagonia to lay eggs each year. It had probably been a nest site for thousands of years.

Iguanodons and nests of eggs

Once they hatched, many dinosaur babies grew quickly. A young *Mamenchisaurus* or *Titanosaurus*, for example, may have put on as much as two tons—four thousand pounds—of weight each year!

Not all dinosaurs had teeth when they hatched. But they may have had what's called an "egg tooth" just as baby birds have at birth. An egg tooth is a sharp pointy tooth on a baby bird's beak. They use it to peck their way out of the eggshells. It falls off a few days after the baby hatches.

Egg tooth

Most dinosaurs laid large numbers of eggs. So even if only a few of the eggs hatched, or only a few babies survived, the species would still continue to exist. That's one reason dinosaurs survived for so many millions of years.

But dinosaurs didn't last forever. Why not?

CHAPTER 7
Wiped Out

No matter where you travel on earth, you will never come across any *T. rexes* or titanosaurs.

So what happened? Why did dinosaurs from prehistoric times become extinct? The truth is that big extinction events—when many life-forms die out all at once—have happened several times in the history of the planet. Most scientists think big extinctions are caused by a giant catastrophe—a terrible event that instantly changes life on earth.

The event that killed the dinosaurs was almost certainly a huge asteroid that crashed into earth about 65 mya. The asteroid was about six to eight miles across—the size of a mountain! It was traveling so fast when it hit earth, it

created a gigantic crater, or dish-shaped hole. The crater is located in Mexico. It's hard to measure the crater because some of it is underwater. But it's at least sixty miles across. When the asteroid hit earth, it caused so much damage that it killed most of the existing life-forms.

How can one asteroid—even a big one—do so much damage all over the globe? For one thing, the force of the asteroid smacking into earth was enormous. It was five billion times as powerful as each of the nuclear bombs that were dropped on Japan at the end of World War II. (Those bombs wiped out two cities in an instant and killed more than two hundred thousand people.) The impact created a dust cloud so big, it may have circled earth in less than an hour. The dust cloud was hot, too. It created a blanket of hot air that started forest fires. Half of the forests on earth may have burned. Many thousands of animals would have been killed in the fires.

The impact of the asteroid was forceful enough to cause the plates in the earth's surface to move. When the plates moved, it set off a series of earthquakes. Volcanoes erupted everywhere. It also triggered huge waves in the ocean, called

tsunamis. The waves drowned out thousands of
life-forms living near the coast.

With the volcanoes erupting in fire and ash,
dinosaurs and all life-forms nearby were killed
and buried in ash. The dust cloud hung in the
sky for so long, it blotted out the sun for months.
The winter was very cold. Plants died without
enough light. Any plant-eating dinosaurs that

survived the impact were doomed to starve to death when the plants died out. When the plant-eaters died, predator dinosaurs had fewer animals to prey on—so they died, too.

Only a few life-forms survived, including crocodiles, small mammals, insects, and birds. Birds were able to move around the globe fast enough to survive the harsh conditions.

Asteroids and Other Space Rocks

Asteroids are giant rocks orbiting the sun. Some of them are many miles across. Meteoroids are smaller rocks flying through space.

When small meteoroids enter earth's atmosphere, they usually burn up and we call them meteors or "shooting stars." But larger meteoroids or asteroids can survive entering earth's atmosphere and hit the ground. Then we change the name and call them meteorites. Thousands of meteorites have hit the earth, but most of them are small. Once in a long while, a meteorite falls on a cow and kills it.

But when an asteroid or large meteorite hits earth, it leaves a big crater—just like the craters that formed the "man in the moon."

Some scientists predict that giant asteroids, big enough to cause an extinction, crash into earth once about every 100 million years. When will the next one hit? The last extinction was 65 million years ago. Do the math. We have another 35 million years to wait.

The Great Dying

Believe it or not, an even bigger mass extinction happened before dinosaurs existed. More than half of all the life on earth was wiped out. Nearly all ocean species were destroyed, and so were most insects. Two-thirds of the land species became extinct. Most plants disappeared. It took at least 10 million years for the earth to recover and once again be filled with a variety of living things. Scientists call this earlier extinction the "Great Dying." It marked the end of the time before dinosaurs came along—and the beginning of the Mesozoic.

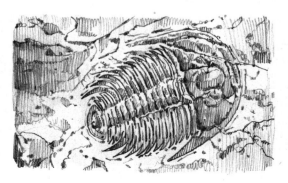

One thing is certain: Whatever destroyed the dinosaurs paved the way for human life on earth. When the Age of the Dinosaurs ended, a new era began—the Age of the Mammals. If the dinosaurs had survived, human beings would probably never have evolved. Earth would be a very different place.

CHAPTER 8
Finding the Bones

The dinosaurs disappeared from the earth 65 million years ago. But their bones were left behind. Over time, some of the bones became buried in layers and layers of dirt and mud. Then the layers hardened into rock. The bones became fossils.

Millions upon millions of years passed. The first modern humans appeared on earth only about two hundred thousand years ago. And only about ten thousand years ago did the first civilizations arise. During all that time, nobody had any idea that the prehistoric world had ever existed. If ancient people found dinosaur bones, they had no idea what they had discovered.

Then, in the seventeenth century, a dinosaur

bone was discovered. It was a huge thigh bone, found in Cornwall, England. The men who found it took it to a professor named Robert Plot. Plot thought about that bone for a long time. What could it be? He knew it was too big to have come from a horse. Could it be from an elephant that someone brought to England hundreds of years ago?

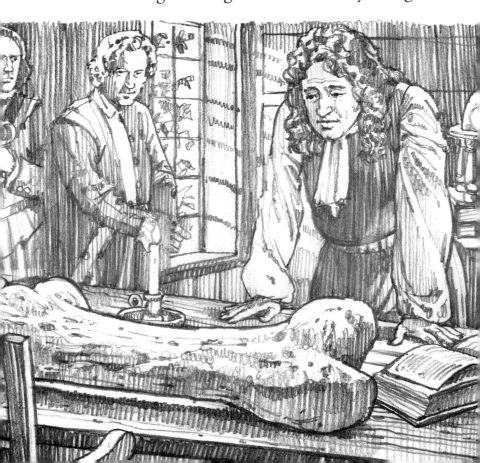

Nope. It was even bigger than an elephant bone. There was only one answer, he decided. It must be from a giant human! That was easier for people to believe than to imagine an animal like a dinosaur.

A hundred years later, more gigantic bones were discovered in England. By 1842, Gideon Mantell had found and named *Iguanodon*. William Buckland had named *Megalosaurus*.

Suddenly, people were very interested in finding more gigantic fossils and unfamiliar bones. But what were these giant creatures? Were they reptiles? Mantell and Buckland looked at the bones and thought they must be giant lizards. After all, *Iguanodon* had the same kind of teeth as an iguana, only bigger.

But slowly, scientists began to think a different way—and they began to understand something amazing. Maybe these weren't merely larger versions of species that still existed. Maybe there were whole species of animals that had lived long ago—but were now gone. Maybe they were animals that had become extinct!

In 1842, a biologist named Richard Owen came up with a name for that group of extinct animals. He called them Dinosauria, which means "terrible lizard."

Richard Owen

Owen was hired to create a display showing the history of the earth. He worked with another man, named Benjamin Waterhouse Hawkins. Together, they created huge hollow sculptures of dinosaurs—or of how Owen thought dinosaurs might have looked. The giant life-size models were put on display in the gardens around London's Crystal Palace. It was a huge glass exhibition hall.

On New Year's Eve in 1853, Owen invited a group of scientists and other important guests to a dinner party. The dinner was held *inside* the giant iguanodon sculpture!

Once the huge dinosaur sculptures were on display in London, people went crazy for dinosaurs. The craze was called "dinomania."

Mary Anning, Girl Dinosaur Hunter
(1799–1847)

Men weren't the only fossil-hunters. A young girl named Mary Anning and her brother Joseph had been trained to hunt for fossils by their father. Mary's family was poor, so they sold the shells and bones to tourists and scientists, to earn money.

When Mary was eleven years old, her father died. Around that time, she and her brother found an entire ichthyosaur skeleton! She continued to collect dinosaur bones her whole life. Scientists would come to her and buy whatever she found. She was the first person to find a fossil of ancient poop! She also found the first complete plesiosaur skeleton discovered in England. She found a pterosaur as well. As an adult, Mary had a deep understanding of the skeletons she uncovered. She knew she was finding unusual species that hadn't been seen before. But Mary was a woman from a poor background—and not educated. Women were not allowed to join the Geological Society of London at that time. So she never got all the credit that she deserved for her discoveries.

Mary Anning

CHAPTER 9
The Bone Wars

By the 1870s and 1880s, dinomania had spread to North America. Hunting for dinosaur bones became serious business. It wasn't just a hobby anymore. It was a battle between fierce competitors—just like *T. rex* and triceratops.

The two American men at the center of the battle were Edward Drinker Cope and Othniel Charles Marsh. They became archrivals. Each

Edward Drinker Cope and Othniel Charles Marsh

man wanted to be the first to find and name the next dinosaur skeleton. Their rivalry became known as the "bone wars."

Marsh was the nephew of a rich man named George Peabody. Edward Drinker Cope came from a wealthy family, too. So both men could afford to travel the world, learning about science and hunting for dinosaur bones.

At first, the two men were friends. But they turned into bitter enemies after Cope found a plesiosaur skeleton.

Cope put it on display in a museum. But when he put the bones together, he put the head on the wrong end! Marsh pointed out the mistake and told everyone about it. After that, the men spent their lives trying to beat each other in finding the best dinosaur bones.

Marsh played many dirty tricks on Cope. Cope had a crew of workers digging, looking for dinosaur bones. But Cope wasn't at the dig site all day. So Marsh paid Cope's workers to give *him* the bones they found, instead of giving them to Cope. Marsh even destroyed some dig sites, rather than let Cope find fossils there!

Marsh found clever ways to get what he wanted. For instance, he made friends with an American Indian chief in the west, Red Cloud, who told him where to look for dinosaur bones. And Marsh bribed workers who were building the railroads across America. They let him know when they found interesting fossils—and made

sure to keep it a secret from Cope.

Cope tried to get back at Marsh by telling newspaper reporters about all the sneaky things Marsh had done.

In the end, both men wound up broke. But that turned out to be a good thing for science.

Cope and Marsh found so many dinosaur fossils because they were working hard to beat each other in the "bone wars." By the time they were done, Marsh had discovered stegosaurus, allosaurus, brontosaurus, and diplodocus—some of the best-known American dinosaurs. Cope had found the first *Coelophysis* (SEE-low-FIE-sis)—a small meat-eater that lived in New Mexico. Many of the skeletons Marsh found are on display in the Peabody Museum of Natural History at Yale University.

Coelophysis

CHAPTER 10
Secrets in the Bones

What can scientists learn about dinosaurs from looking at the fossils found by Marsh, Cope, and others? From the fossils, scientists can figure out how dinosaurs moved, how much they ate, how much they weighed, and how fast they could run.

To find out how fast dinosaurs moved, paleontologists look at trackways. Trackways are fossil footprints preserved in stone. If the footprints are far apart, the dinosaur was either large or running fast—or both. Large, deep footprints tell us how much a dinosaur might have weighed.

Trackways reveal other secrets about dinosaur life, too. They tell us whether dinosaurs roamed around alone or in groups. From trackways, paleontologists can guess that the biggest dinosaurs—such as brachiosaurs, diplodocus, and brontosaurus—may have lived in herds. But the herds were sometimes separated by age. The adults formed one group while the younger dinosaurs formed another.

Why?

These gigantic plant-eaters had to spend so much time eating, in order to grow so big. Perhaps a younger diplodocus couldn't reach the tall trees where the adults were feeding. It wouldn't make sense for the younger dinos to hang out with their parents, if they couldn't reach the food.

Besides studying trackways, paleontologists can tell how fast dinosaurs moved by looking at the way their leg joints fit together. Their legs had to be flexible in order to move quickly. From the skeletons, we know that many dinosaurs could rear up on their hind legs, like a horse! And many dinosaurs could run fast enough so that all their feet were off the ground at the same time. *T. rex* could probably run at least sixteen miles per hour.

Brachiosaurus eating

How Old Is That Dinosaur?

Paleontologists can tell when a dinosaur lived by looking at fossils—and at the layers of rocks where the dino fossil was found.

Triassic, Jurassic, and Cretaceous are the names of time periods. But they are also the names of layers of rocks on the earth's surface. Each layer of rock has fossils in it, so each layer tells the story of the history of the earth.

Cretaceous

Jurassic

Triassic

The top layer is the most recent. But if you dig down into the earth, you find layers of rock that are much older. The fossils in the rocks show what kinds of plants and animals lived in the past. The deeper you go, the older the rocks are, because the layers have been building up over time.

To help figure out exactly when a certain dinosaur lived, paleontologists try to find what they call "index fossils" buried in the same layer of rock with the dinosaur. An index fossil is a fossil of some other species that only lived during a certain era. For example, there might be a small ocean creature—a fish or a frog—that only lived during a few million years in the Jurassic period. If a frog is found in the same rock layer where they find a dinosaur, then both species must have lived at the same time.

Skeletons tell us that many dinosaurs had large nasal openings, so they probably had a good sense of smell. Their eye sockets were often large, so they probably had good eyesight, like birds. From the bones, we know that some dinosaurs had flexible, whiplike tails. Others had rigid tails that helped them keep their balance. Most of them carried their tails up, parallel to the ground. They didn't drag them.

Dinosaurs had flexible arms. In some, like *Zhenyuanlong suni*, their arms evolved into wings! Others were able to move their arms sideways. They could reach out and quickly snatch their prey.

By studying teeth and body structure, scientists can tell what a dinosaur was likely to eat. Did it have huge jaws, sharp pointy teeth, and powerful clawlike hands? Then it was probably a gigantic killing machine, built to attack other animals and eat the prey.

Dinosaur bones tell us just about everything we know about these ancient animals.

They also tell us one more incredible thing—that some dinosaurs are still alive today!

CHAPTER 11
Are Dinosaurs Really Extinct?

Is it possible that dinosaurs are still living today? It's not only possible—it's absolutely true. All the prehistoric dinosaurs that you've heard about died out completely 65 million years ago. But flying dinosaurs are still here today. They are called birds!

That's right. Strange as it may seem, scientists have realized that birds are actually dinosaurs. Why? Because they both evolved from the very same ancestors.

Scientists put all living things into groups or classes. They decide which group a species belongs in based on its physical traits. One big group, or superclass, are called tetrapods—animals that have a backbone and four limbs. But that's a

huge group! It includes everything from turtles to horses to people. So scientists break the big groups into smaller ones. Mammals are one of the smaller groups. Dinosaurs are another.

Did Dinosaurs Make Sounds?

That's a hard question to answer just by looking at bones. Scientists can only guess—and they base their guesses on the other animals that are similar to dinosaurs. Since birds are so closely related to dinosaurs, and birds make sounds, it's possible that dinosaurs did, too. But dinosaurs are also closely related to reptiles. Most reptiles make no vocal sounds. Some scientists think some dinosaurs could make a sound by breathing through the crests on their head—sort of like blowing through a horn! The best guess is that dinosaurs might have made some sound, but probably not much.

It might seem odd to say that birds are dinosaurs, but birds and dinosaurs have a lot in common. They both have hollow bones. They both lay eggs. Birds have feathers, as did some dinosaurs.

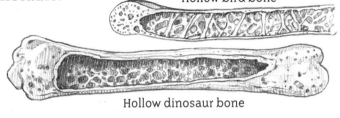

Hollow bird bone

Hollow dinosaur bone

It's amazing to think that some creatures survived when the asteroid hit earth, 65 million years ago. But it's not surprising. Birds didn't need to eat as much as the dinosaurs needed—and they could fly away. Flying helped birds hunt for food. It also helped them escape the worst part of the disaster. Other small animals survived, too.

So the next time you want to see a creature that lived when the dinosaurs lived, just look up in the sky. There's probably a dinosaur flying over you right now.

Jurassic, the Movies

In 1993, a movie called *Jurassic Park* came out. It was based on a book by Michael Crichton. The movie was such a huge success that three more movies were filmed. More are planned for the future. Video

games, toys, and T-shirts based on *Jurassic Park* all became popular. Everyone loved the idea behind the movie. Wouldn't it be amazing if someone could clone dinosaurs and put them in a theme park?

But the movies weren't accurate. For one thing, it's believed to be impossible to clone dinosaurs. Headlines about cloning dinosaurs were made in 2016 when the remains of a pregnant *T. rex* were found in Montana. This led some science writers to wonder whether the pregnant *T. rex* had usable DNA. (DNA is the code in living cells that instructs a creature how to grow.) But DNA is known to decay after a few hundred years. So it's unlikely that a dinosaur could be cloned.

Also, the movies show huge velociraptors. In real life, velociraptors were much smaller, and they probably had feathers. The creatures shown in the movies were more like a dinosaur called *Deinonychus*.

It's an honor to have a dinosaur species named for you. Originally a dinosaur found in Utah was going to be named for Steven Spielberg, the director of the first *Jurassic Park* movie. The dino would have

Steven Spielberg

been called *Utahraptor spielbergi* (YOO-tah-RAP-tor speel-BURG-ee). Scientists hoped that Spielberg would donate money to dinosaur research. When he didn't, they named the new dinosaur for two other people instead. One was a scientist. The other was a man who made dinosaur models for zoos and museums.

Timeline of the Age of the Dinosaurs

252 mya	The Great Dying
250 mya–200 mya	Triassic period
230 mya	First dinosaurs appear
200 mya–145 mya	Jurassic period
145 mya–65 mya	Cretaceous period
65 mya	Mass extinction of dinosaurs
AD 1670s	Dinosaur thigh bone found in England
1810–1811	Mary Anning finds an entire ichthyosaur skeleton
1822	Gideon Mantell finds teeth of *Iguanodon*
1842	Richard Owen creates the name Dinosauria
1853	Dinner party in the iguanodon sculpture at the Crystal Palace
1870s–1880s	Dinomania spreads to North America
	Bone wars of Cope and Marsh
1993	Movie *Jurassic Park* comes out
2011	Bones of a new kind of titanosaur excavated in Patagonia
2015	Movie *Jurassic World* released
2016	Titanosaur skeleton unveiled at the American Museum of Natural History in New York City

Timeline of the World

4,567 mya	Formation of the solar system
4,500 mya	Formation of the earth
3,000 mya	Ancestor of all animals, plants, and fungi appears
375 mya	Vertebrates with legs appear
125 mya	Flowering plants appear
45 mya	Modern mammal groups are present
200,000 years ago	Modern humans appear
71,000 years ago	Invention of the bow and arrow
5,500 years ago	Invention of the wheel
1500 BC	Bronze Age farming culture covers most of Europe
594 BC	Rise of democracy in Greece
AD 105	Paper made in China
1760	Industrial Revolution begins
1776	American War for Independence begins
1814	George Stephenson builds the first practical steam locomotive
1869	American Museum of Natural History founded
1945	Atomic Age begins with the first nuclear explosion
1957	Space Age begins with the launch of *Sputnik*
1989	World Wide Web invented
2007	Apple releases the first iPhone

Bibliography

*Books for young readers

*Morgan, Ben, and Caroline Bingham, ed. *Dinosaurs: A Visual Encyclopedia*. New York: DK Publishing, 2011.

Paul, Gregory S. *The Princeton Field Guide to Dinosaurs*. Princeton, NJ: Princeton University Press, 2010.

Paul, Gregory S., ed. *The Scientific American Book of Dinosaurs*. New York: St. Martin's Press, 2000.

Pim, Keiron. *Dinosaurs—The Grand Tour*. New York: The Experiment, 2014.

Sir Richard Owen, the English paleontologist who
coined the word *Dinosauria*—meaning "terrible lizard"

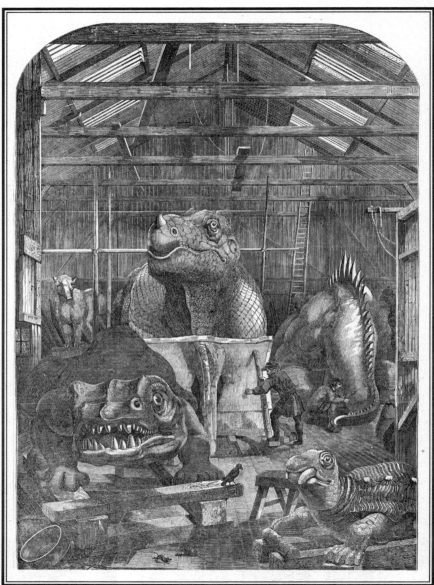

An illustration of the extinct animals model room
at the Crystal Palace, England, 1853

The models today in Crystal Palace Park, London, England

Courtesy of the Peabody Museum of Natural History, Yale University

Othniel Charles Marsh (center, back row) with his excavation crew, 1872

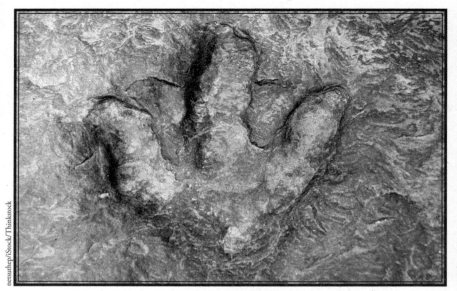

A dinosaur footprint in Thailand

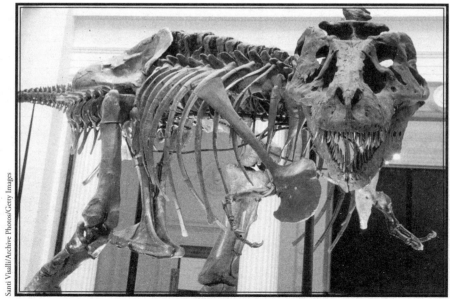

A *Tyrannosaurus rex* fossil skeleton on display at the
Field Museum of Natural History, Chicago

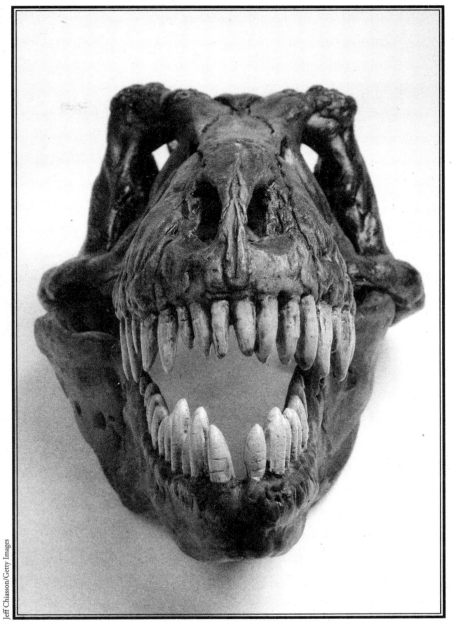

The skull of a *Tyrannosaurus rex*

A titanosaur replica at the American Museum of
Natural History, New York City

A replica of a *Utahraptor* fossil skeleton at the
North American Museum of Ancient Life, Utah

A triceratops skull fossil at the American Museum of
Natural History, New York City

A stegosaurus skeleton fossil

Baby dinosaur fossils from Mongolia

An ichthyosaur fossil

Cast of *Apatosaurus excelsus* at the Tellus Science Museum, Cartersville, Georgia

A fossilized dinosaur nest

Paleontologist working on a *Tyrannosaurus rex* fossil